My Family Tree Research Records

A Family Tree Research Workbook

Written by Catherine Coulter

Other Books Written By Catherine Coulter

My Family Tree Research Records

Family Group Research Records

Census Research Records

Cemetery and Funeral Home Research Records

Court House Research Records

Web Log and Web Accounts

Books Written by Catherine Coulter under the name of Cathy Coulter

The Man in Red

A Children's Book of Poems Goodnight and Hello

My Family Tree Research Records: A Family Tree Research Workbook

Copyright © 2013 Catherine Coulter
All Rights Reserved
ISBN-13: 978-1482570281
ISBN-10: 1482570289

Content Page

My Ancestors in This Workbook
How to Begin
Records and Documents to Research

Chapter 1
　　Cover Research Check List for Individual Ancestors
　　Family Research Record

Chapter 2
　　Census Logs

Chapter 3
　　Cemetery
　　Funeral Home

Chapter 4
　　Birth
　　Marriage
　　Death
　　Naturalization
　　Land/Deed

Chapter 5
　　Military Records

Chapter 6
　　Library Research
　　List Books to Check Out

Chapter 7
　　Web Log
　　Web Accounts
　　Web Sites to Consider

Ancestors in this Workbook

Ancestor's Names	Chapter Numbers

Introduction

Each chapter in <u>My Family Tree Research Records</u> is designed to help you with your research whether you are on the internet, traveling to a historical society, or any place your research leads you. The chapters contain information that will help with the different kinds of records you may find yourself working with, such as census records, court house records, and more.

Before starting your research, add any information you already know about the ancestors you are looking for into the workbook. This information will come in handy when you are doing your research. It will be all in one place and organized. There will be no more lost or out of order pages. This workbook, pen, post it flags, camera, and an empty legal sized folder to hold any photo copies you obtain, makes an easy portable research kit. Multiple file folders of information on each ancestor will not be needed.

There are check lists of the many kinds of information related to the family tree research and web site logs to help keep track of which web sites you find useful and to help keep track of where you have found your information. The web site log will also be able to be used for citing the documents and records you find.

You can place tabs on the first page of each chapter to help you find them faster. There are also blank pages throughout this book for taking notes and planning your research. If you should decide to use this workbook for one surname then you could add that surname on the cover of this book as well.

How to Begin

The best place to start your family tree is with yourself and work backward, because you know the most information about yourself. Each generation as you go backward will give you clues on where to look for information on the next generation. It is very much like a puzzle with the pieces scattered on the floor. You never know for sure which piece you will find next and how it will lead to the next puzzle piece being found. But in the end you will have a nice picture of your family tree.

Talking to relatives can be a big source of information and family stories which are always interesting and full of information that could help you in your research. But please keep in mind that stories over time have the tendency to unintentionally change a little or some facts to be lost. It's best to verify facts with documents and such if you can. For example, a story in our family said that two boys were twins and born in America. I was looking for the twin boys in America and I could not find them. I had though been able to verify the rest of the story. I did not give up on finding them. It was not until I found the ship list that had our family on it that I discovered the boys were not twins but born one year apart in Wales. If I had insisted they were twins because of the family story I never would have found them. So keep an open mind and verify your facts whether it is from a family story, from message boards or someone else's family tree. Unintentional mistakes can be made as easy as a flip in numbers (45 instead of a 54).

At some point you will hit a brick wall. A point when you just cannot find information on an ancestor or an ancestor themselves. Its ok, everyone has those times and do not let yourself give up and end it there. You will find a way around or over that wall given time. I find, for me, that if I leave the family I have hit the brick wall with and work on another branch for a while, that when I go back to the first one I have fresh eyes and a different approach to the problem. I then more often find things that I would never have the first time. I like to think of the old saying that goes something like try, try, and try again.

Note that not every ancestor will use his or her first name. There are some ancestors that preferred to use their middle name instead of their first name for many reasons. One reason is to distinguish themselves from another family member with the same name. Usually someone they are named after such as a parent or grandparent. A second reason could be that maybe it was used as an endearment from a loved one. A third reason could be that they just did not like their first name for some reason. I have a branch of my family that I found the hard way that for several generations the men used their middle names in census records and other documents then their first name on other documents still. So when searching, keep in mind any middle names you may find for your ancestors.

You may need to consider nicknames if you are having trouble finding an ancestor. There are many reasons a nickname is used instead of their given name.

Like in the above paragraph, they may not like their given name but decide that a different version or nickname was better. You should be aware of the various nicknames and versions of your ancestor's names because of this. For example, an ancestor by the name of Robert could be using the name Bert, Rob, or Bob instead. A web site by the Connecticut State Library has a listing of possible American nicknames of the 18th and 19th Century for both males and females at www.cslib.org/nickname.htm. The US Gen Web site also has a list of common nick names for males and females at www.usgenweb.org/research/nicknames.shtml. These sites may be useful to you in your research.

Another thing that can hinder your research is the spelling of names. There are many reasons for the change in how a name was spelled. A name may have been spelled wrong during the creation of a document. For example, a census enumerator spelled it as he thought it should be spelled and got it wrong due to your ancestor's accent or how the name sounded. Also there were times when your ancestor may have changed his own name in order to Americanize it, to fit in, or even to sound less like their nationality or other reasons. It is not only last names that may have changed in the way they were spelled their first names could have been affected as well.

I have found that sometimes the way people wrote affected the spellings of names when transcribed. The trouble could be as simple as hand writing being poor or even as elaborate enough to be confusing. I have seen what was supposed to be a capital **C** look like a **G**. I also have an ancestor that we believed his name was Samuel because of the hand writing that was used and later found out that his name was really Lemuel.

Make sure you verify and document your findings. Verifying will help insure that your information you found is accurate. Document your information by writing down the details of the web site, book, or other source where you have found your information. You never know when you may need to look up that information again or want to search it some more. It will also let others find it as well. Verifying and documenting you information will also give your information credibility and the assurance to others that it is accurate.

List of Records and Documents to Research

- ☐ Baptism
- ☐ Birth Records
- ☐ Books
- ☐ Cemetery
- ☐ Census Records
- ☐ Children
- ☐ Church Records
- ☐ City Directories
- ☐ Death
- ☐ Divorce Records
- ☐ Family Stories
- ☐ Historical Landmarks
- ☐ Historical Societies
- ☐ Immigration
- ☐ Jobs
- ☐ Land Deeds
- ☐ Land Grants
- ☐ Library's
- ☐ Marriage Records
- ☐ Military Records
- ☐ Mortality Schedules
- ☐ National Archives
- ☐ National Battle Fields
- ☐ National Parks
- ☐ Naturalization
- ☐ Newspapers
- ☐ Obituaries
- ☐ Photos
- ☐ Probate
- ☐ Tax Lists
- ☐ Voting Lists

- ☐ Web Sites
- ☐ Will
- ☐ Immigration
- ☐ Ship Lists / Records
- ☐ Port of Departure
- ☐ Port of Entry
- ☐ Castle Garden Years of 1855 to 1890
- ☐ Ellis Island Years of 1892 to 1954
- ☐ Other Immigrant Landing Ports
- ☐ Canada Boarder
- ☐ Mexico Boarder
- ☐ Wars
- ☐ Adoption
- ☐ Migration
- ☐ Funeral
- ☐ Education
- ☐ _____
- ☐ _____
- ☐ _____
- ☐ _____
- ☐ _____
- ☐ _____
- ☐ _____
- ☐ _____
- ☐ _____
- ☐ _____
- ☐ _____
- ☐ _____

Chapter One

List of Records and Documents to Research

The list of records and documents to research is a check list to help you keep track of the many kinds of documents and records that you may want to research for your family. It leaves several lines blank for you to fill in any others that you can think of that are not already there or for any notations you wish to make.

Cover Research Check List

In this book you will find a Cover Research Check List to go along with each family group record. This check list will help keep track of what you have searched for that particular ancestor and what you have not. Just place an X in the box for any records that do not apply to your ancestor. Then place a √ check mark in the box for the records you have found for this ancestor as you fill in the information on the following family group record. There is a space for notes at the end of this list in case you would like to write a few planning notes, contact names or other places to search. It is a fast and easy way to plan your research needs.

Family Group Research Record

A family group record is a great research tool for you to take on research trips to the library, historical societies, and anywhere your research takes you. Using a family group research record will help you organize your information and prepare it to be entered into a computer program, book, or chart. It will also show you what information is missing and what you have. At the end, there is a place for notes or sources to be added as well. It is a good idea to list the sources of your information so you can access them again if you need to or just to let you know what you have already accessed.

You will find in these family group records that there is plenty of room for you to write in your information without it being cramped or hard to read. It includes the usual information such as name of ancestor, dates, and notes for the following information: birth, death, buried, parents, marriages, spouses, and up to 20 children with their birth dates, death dates, and places they were born. The family group record also includes a place for each year of the census from 1790 to 1940. The census section has a place for the state, county, township, and notes for each year. There is a space for notes as well at the end of the group record. It also has spaces for religion, occupation, military, and residences. You can fill in the blank space I left for other facts you may find.

Cover Research Check List For

- ☐ Birth:
  - o Family Mentioned Info
  - o Certificate
  - o Church Record
  - o Newspaper
  - o County Court Records
  - o Historical Society
  - o Cemetery Record
  - o Census Record
  - o Adoption
- ☐ Baptism
  - o Family Mentioned Info
  - o Certificate
  - o Church Record
  - o Newspaper
  - o County Court Records
  - o Historical Society
  - o Cemetery Record
- ☐ Marriage#_____
  - o Family Mentioned Info
  - o Certificate
  - o Church Record
  - o Newspaper
  - o County Court Records
  - o Historical Society
  - o Cemetery Record
  - o Census Record
  - o Children
- ☐ Divorce#_____
  - o Family Info Certificate
  - o Newspaper
  - o County Court Records
  - o Historical Society
  - o Census Record

- ☐ Military
  - o War
  - o Family Info
  - o Newspaper
  - o Historical Society
  - o Nation Archives
  - o Draft Registration
  - o Pension Record
- ☐ Census Records
  - o 1790
  - o 1800
  - o 1810
  - o 1820
  - o 1830
  - o 1840
  - o 1850
  - o 1860
  - o 1870
  - o 1880
  - o 1890
  - o 1900
  - o 1910
  - o 1920
  - o 1930
  - o 1940
  - o 1950
  - o 1960
- ☐ Death Record
  - o Family Mentioned
  - o Mortality Schedules
- ☐ Mortality Schedules
- ☐ Obituaries
- ☐ Funeral Home Records
- ☐ Cemetery Records
- ☐ Court Records
- ☐ Wills
- ☐ Probate Records
- ☐ Immigration
  - o Ship Lists/ Records
  - o Port of Departure
  - o Port of Entry
  - o Newspapers
  - o Castle Garden Records

- - -
    - Ellis Island Records
    - Records of Other Immigrant landing Ports
    - Border Crossing
  - ☐ Naturalization
    - Court Records
    - Certificate of Citizenship
    - Census Records
- ☐ Cemetery
- ☐ Church
- ☐ City Directories
- ☐ Education
- ☐ Family Stories About Ancestor
- ☐ Funeral Home

- ☐ Land Grants / Deeds
- ☐ Migration
- ☐ Newspapers
- ☐ Obituary
- ☐ Occupation
- ☐ Photos
- ☐ Tax List
- ☐ Voter Lists
- ☐ Will / Probate
- ☐ _____
- ☐ _____
- ☐ _____
- ☐ _____
- ☐ _____

Ancestor's Name _____

Event	Month	Day	Year	Notes	Note #
Born					
Died					
Buried					
Father B.					
D.					
Mother B.					
D.					
Married 1					
Spouse 1 B.					
D.					
Married 2					
Spouse 2 B.					
D.					
Religion					
Occupation					
Military					
Residence					
Residence					

Children:

	Name	Date of Birth	Place of Birth	Death Date
1.				
2.				
3.				
4.				
5.				
6.				
7.				
8.				
9.				

Children Continued:

#	Name	Date of Birth	Place of Birth	Death Date
10.				
12.				
13.				
14.				
15.				
16.				
18.				
19.				
20.				

U.S. Federal Census

	State	County	Township	Notes
1790				
1800				
1810				
1820				
1830				
1840				
1850				
1860				
1870				
1880				
1890				
1900				
1910				
1920				
1930				

Notes/Source (Remember to number the note /source and link it to the above so you can find it faster.)

Cover Research Check List For

- ☐ Birth:
  - o Family Mentioned Info
  - o Certificate
  - o Church Record
  - o Newspaper
  - o County Court Records
  - o Historical Society
  - o Cemetery Record
  - o Census Record
  - o Adoption
- ☐ Baptism
  - o Family Mentioned Info
  - o Certificate
  - o Church record
  - o Newspaper
  - o County Court records
  - o Historical society
  - o Cemetery record
- ☐ Marriage#_____
  - o Family Mentioned Info
  - o Certificate
  - o Church Record
  - o Newspaper
  - o County Court Records
  - o Historical Society
  - o Cemetery Record
  - o Census Record
  - o Children
- ☐ Divorce#_____
  - o Family Info Certificate
  - o Newspaper
  - o County Court Records
  - o Historical Society
  - o Census Record
- ☐ Military
  - o War
  - o Family Info
  - o Newspaper
  - o Historical Society
  - o Nation Archives
  - o Draft Registration
  - o Pension Record
- ☐ Census Records
  - o 1790
  - o 1800
  - o 1810
  - o 1820
  - o 1830
  - o 1840
  - o 1850
  - o 1860
  - o 1870
  - o 1880
  - o 1890
  - o 1900
  - o 1910
  - o 1920
  - o 1930
  - o 1940
  - o 1950
  - o 1960
- ☐ Death Record
  - o Family Mentioned
  - o Mortality Schedules
- ☐ Mortality Schedules
- ☐ Obituaries
- ☐ Funeral Home Records
- ☐ Cemetery Records
- ☐ Court Records
- ☐ Wills
- ☐ Probate Records
- ☐ Immigration
  - o Ship Lists/ Records
  - o Port of Departure
  - o Port of Entry
  - o Newspapers
  - o Castle Garden Records
  - o Ellis Island Records

- - o Records of Other Immigrant Landing Ports
  - o Border Crossing
  - ☐ Naturalization
    - o Court Records
    - o Certificate of Citizenship
    - o Census Records
- ☐ Cemetery
- ☐ Church
- ☐ City Directories
- ☐ Education
- ☐ Family Stories About Ancestor
- ☐ Funeral Home
- ☐ Land Grants / Deeds
- ☐ Migration
- ☐ Newspapers
- ☐ Obituary
- ☐ Occupation
- ☐ Photos
- ☐ Tax List
- ☐ Voter Lists
- ☐ Will / Probate
- ☐ _____
- ☐ _____
- ☐ _____
- ☐ _____
- ☐ _____

Ancestor's Name _____

Event	Month	Day	Year	Notes	Note #
Born					
Died					
Buried					
Father B.					
D.					
Mother B.					
D.					
Married 1					
Spouse 1B.					
D.					
Married 2					
Spouse 2 B.					
D.					
Religion					
Occupation					
Military					
Residence					
Residence					

Children:

	Name	Date of Birth	Place of Birth	Death Date
1.				
2.				
3.				
4.				
5.				
6.				
7.				
8.				
9.				

Children continued:

	Name	Date of Birth	Place of Birth	Death Date
10.				
12.				
13.				
14.				
15.				
16.				
18.				
19.				
20.				

U.S. Federal Census

	State	County	Township	Notes
1790				
1800				
1810				
1820				
1830				
1840				
1850				
1860				
1870				
1880				
1890				
1900				
1910				
1920				
1930				

Notes/Source (Remember to number the note /source and link it to the above so you can find it faster.)

Cover Research Check List for

- ☐ Birth:
    - o Family Mentioned Info
    - o Certificate
    - o Church Record
    - o Newspaper
    - o County Court Records
    - o Historical society
    - o Cemetery Record
    - o Census Record
    - o Adoption
- ☐ *Baptism*
    - o Family Mentioned Info
    - o Certificate
    - o Church Record
    - o Newspaper
    - o County Court Records
    - o Historical Society
    - o Cemetery Record
- ☐ Marriage#_____
    - o Family Mentioned Info
    - o Certificate
    - o Church Record
    - o Newspaper
    - o County Court Records
    - o Historical Society
    - o Cemetery Record
    - o Census Record
    - o Children
- ☐ Divorce#_____
    - o Family Info Certificate
    - o Newspaper
    - o County Court Records
    - o Historical Society
    - o Census Record
- ☐ Military
    - o War
    - o Family Info
    - o Newspaper
    - o Historical Society
    - o Nation Archives
    - o Draft Registration
    - o Pension Record
- ☐ Census Records
    - o 1790
    - o 1800
    - o 1810
    - o 1820
    - o 1830
    - o 1840
    - o 1850
    - o 1860
    - o 1870
    - o 1880
    - o 1890
    - o 1900
    - o 1910
    - o 1920
    - o 1930
    - o 1940
    - o 1950
    - o 1960
- ☐ Death Record
    - o Family Mentioned In
    - o Mortality Schedules
- ☐ Mortality Schedules
- ☐ Obituaries
- ☐ Funeral home Records
- ☐ Cemetery Records
- ☐ Court Records
- ☐ Wills
- ☐ Probate Records
- ☐ Immigration
    - o Ship Lists/ Records
    - o Port of Departure
    - o Port of Entry
    - o Newspapers
    - o Castle Garden Records
    - o Ellis Island Records

- Records of Other Immigrant Landing Ports
- Border crossing
- ☐ Naturalization
  - Court Records
  - Certificate of Citizenship
  - Census Records
- ☐ Cemetery
- ☐ Church
- ☐ City Directories
- ☐ Education
- ☐ Family Stories About Ancestor
- ☐ Funeral Home
- ☐ Land Grants / Deeds

- ☐ Migration
- ☐ Newspapers
- ☐ Obituary
- ☐ Occupation
- ☐ Photos
- ☐ Tax List
- ☐ Voter Lists
- ☐ Will / Probate
- ☐ _____
- ☐ _____
- ☐ _____
- ☐ _____
- ☐ _____

Ancestor's Name _____

Event	Month	Day	Year	Notes	Note #
Born					
Died					
Buried					
Father B.					
D.					
Mother B.					
D.					
Married 1					
Spouse 1B.					
D.					
Married 2					
Spouse 2 B.					
D.					
Religion					
Occupation					
Military					
Residence					
Residence					

Children:	Name	Date of Birth	Place of Birth	Death Date
1.				
2.				
3.				
4.				
5.				
6.				
7.				
8.				
9.				

Children Continued:

#	Name	Date of Birth	Place of Birth	Death Date
10.				
12.				
13.				
14.				
15.				
16.				
18.				
19.				
20.				

U.S. Federal Census

Year	State	County	Township	Notes
1790				
1800				
1810				
1820				
1830				
1840				
1850				
1860				
1870				
1880				
1890				
1900				
1910				
1920				
1930				

Notes/Source (Remember to number the note /source and link it to the above so you can find it faster.)

Cover Research Check list for

- ☐ Birth:
    - o Family Mentioned Info
    - o Certificate
    - o Church Record
    - o Newspaper
    - o County Court Records
    - o Historical Society
    - o Cemetery Record
    - o Census Record
    - o Adoption
- ☐ Baptism
    - o Family Mentioned Info
    - o Certificate
    - o Church Record
    - o Newspaper
    - o County Court Records
    - o Historical Society
    - o Cemetery Record
- ☐ Marriage#_____
    - o Family Mentioned Info
    - o Certificate
    - o Church Record
    - o Newspaper
    - o County Court Records
    - o Historical Society
    - o Cemetery Record
    - o Census Record
    - o Children
- ☐ Divorce#_____
    - o Family info Certificate
    - o Newspaper
    - o County Court Records
    - o Historical Society
    - o Census Record
- ☐ Military
    - o War
    - o Family Info
    - o Newspaper
    - o Historical Society
    - o Nation Archives
    - o Draft Registration
    - o Pension Record
- ☐ Census Records
    - o 1790
    - o 1800
    - o 1810
    - o 1820
    - o 1830
    - o 1840
    - o 1850
    - o 1860
    - o 1870
    - o 1880
    - o 1890
    - o 1900
    - o 1910
    - o 1920
    - o 1930
    - o 1940
    - o 1950
    - o 1960
- ☐ Death Record
    - o Family Mentioned In
    - o Mortality Schedules
- ☐ Mortality Schedules
- ☐ Obituaries
- ☐ Funeral Home Records
- ☐ Cemetery Records
- ☐ Court Records
- ☐ Wills
- ☐ Probate Records
- ☐ Immigration
    - o Ship Lists/ Records
    - o Port of Departure
    - o Port of Entry
    - o Newspapers
    - o Castle Garden Records
    - o Ellis Island Records

- o Records of Other Immigrant Landing Ports
- o Border Crossing
- ☐ Naturalization
  - o Court Records
  - o Certificate of Citizenship
  - o Census Records
- ☐ Cemetery
- ☐ Church
- ☐ City Directories
- ☐ Education
- ☐ Family Stories About Ancestor
- ☐ Funeral Home

- ☐ Land Grants / Deeds
- ☐ Migration
- ☐ Newspapers
- ☐ Obituary
- ☐ Occupation
- ☐ Photos
- ☐ Tax List
- ☐ Voter Lists
- ☐ Will / Probate
- ☐ _____
- ☐ _____
- ☐ _____
- ☐ _____

Ancestor's Name _____

Event	Month	Day	Year	Notes	Note #
Born					
Died					
Buried					
Father B.					
D.					
Mother B.					
D.					
Married 1					
Spouse 1 B.					
D.					
Married 2					
Spouse 2 B.					
D.					
Religion					
Occupation					
Military					
Residence					
Residence					

Children:

#	Name	Date of Birth	Place of Birth	Death Date
1.				
2.				
3.				
4.				
5.				
6.				
7.				
8.				
9.				

Children Continued:

	Name	Date of Birth	Place of Birth	Death Date
10.				
12.				
13.				
14.				
15.				
16.				
18.				
19.				
20.				

U.S. Federal Census

	State	County	Township	Notes
1790				
1800				
1810				
1820				
1830				
1840				
1850				
1860				
1870				
1880				
1890				
1900				
1910				
1920				
1930				

Notes/Source (Remember to number the note /source and link it to the above so you can find it faster.)

Cover Research Check list for

- ☐ Birth:
  - o Family Mentioned Info
  - o Certificate
  - o Church Record
  - o Newspaper
  - o County Court Records
  - o Historical Society
  - o Cemetery Record
  - o Census Record
  - o Adoption
- ☐ Baptism
  - o Family Mentioned Info
  - o Certificate
  - o Church Record
  - o Newspaper
  - o County Court Records
  - o Historical Society
  - o Cemetery Record
- ☐ Marriage#_____
  - o Family Mentioned Info Certificate
  - o Church Record
  - o Newspaper
  - o County Court Records
  - o Historical Society
  - o Cemetery Record
  - o Census Record
  - o Children
- ☐ Divorce#_____
  - o Family Info Certificate
  - o Newspaper
  - o County Court Records
  - o Historical Society
  - o Census Record

- ☐ Military
  - o War
  - o Family Info
  - o Newspaper
  - o Historical Society
  - o Nation Archives
  - o Draft Registration
  - o Pension Record
- ☐ Census Records
  - o 1790
  - o 1800
  - o 1810
  - o 1820
  - o 1830
  - o 1840
  - o 1850
  - o 1860
  - o 1870
  - o 1880
  - o 1890
  - o 1900
  - o 1910
  - o 1920
  - o 1930
  - o 1940
  - o 1950
  - o 1960
- ☐ Death Record
  - o Family Mentioned In
  - o Mortality Schedules
- ☐ Mortality Schedules
- ☐ Obituaries
- ☐ Funeral Home Records
- ☐ Cemetery Records
- ☐ Court Records
- ☐ Wills
- ☐ Probate Records
- ☐ Immigration
  - o Ship lists/ Records
  - o Port of Departure
  - o Port of Entry
  - o Newspapers
  - o Castle Garden Records
  - o Ellis Island Records

- - o Records of Other Immigrant landing Ports
  - o Border Crossing
  - Naturalization
    - o Court Records
    - o Certificate of Citizenship
    - o Census Records
- Cemetery
- Church
- City Directories
- Education
- Family Stories About Ancestor
- Funeral Home
- Land Grants / Deeds

- Migration
- Newspapers
- Obituary
- Occupation
- Photos
- Tax List
- Voter Lists
- Will / Probate
- _____
- _____
- _____
- _____
- _____

Ancestor's Name _____

Event	Month	Day	Year	Notes	Note #
Born					
Died					
Buried					
Father B.					
D.					
Mother B.					
D.					
Married 1					
Spouse 1 B.					
D.					
Married 2					
Spouse 2 B.					
D.					
Religion					
Occupation					
Military					
Residence					
Residence					

Children:

	Name	Date of Birth	Place of Birth	Death Date
1.				
2.				
3.				
4.				
5.				
6.				
7.				
8.				
9.				

Children Continued:

	Name	Date of Birth	Place of Birth	Death Date
10.				
12.				
13.				
14.				
15.				
16.				
18.				
19.				
20.				

U.S. Federal Census

	State	County	Township	Notes
1790				
1800				
1810				
1820				
1830				
1840				
1850				
1860				
1870				
1880				
1890				
1900				
1910				
1920				
1930				

Notes/Source (Remember to number the note /source and link it to the above so you can find it faster.)

Cover Research Check List for

- ☐ Birth:
    - o Family Mentioned Info
    - o Certificate
    - o Church Record
    - o Newspaper
    - o County Court Records
    - o Historical Society
    - o Cemetery Record
    - o Census Record
    - o Adoption
- ☐ Baptism
    - o Family Mentioned Info
    - o Certificate
    - o Church Record
    - o Newspaper
    - o County Court Records
    - o Historical Society
    - o Cemetery Record
- ☐ Marriage#_____
    - o Family Mentioned Info
    - o Certificate
    - o Church Record Newspaper
    - o County Court Record
    - o Historical Society
    - o Cemetery Record
    - o Census Record
    - o Children
- ☐ Divorce#_____
    - o Family Info Certificate
    - o Newspaper
    - o County Court Records
    - o Historical Society
    - o Census Record

- ☐ Military
    - o War
    - o Family Info
    - o Newspaper
    - o Historical Society
    - o Nation Archives
    - o Draft Registration
    - o Pension Record
- ☐ Census Records
    - o 1790
    - o 1800
    - o 1810
    - o 1820
    - o 1830
    - o 1840
    - o 1850
    - o 1860
    - o 1870
    - o 1880
    - o 1890
    - o 1900
    - o 1910
    - o 1920
    - o 1930
    - o 1940
    - o 1950
    - o 1960
- ☐ Death Record
    - o Family Mentioned In
    - o Mortality Schedules
- ☐ Mortality Schedules
- ☐ Obituaries
- ☐ Funeral Home Records
- ☐ Cemetery Records
- ☐ Court Records
- ☐ Wills
- ☐ Probate Records
- ☐ Immigration
    - o Ship Lists/ Records
    - o Port of Departure
    - o Port of Entry
    - o Newspapers
    - o Castle Garden Records
    - o Ellis Island Records

-
  -
    - Records of Other Immigrant Landing Ports
    - Border Crossing
  - Naturalization
    - Court Records
    - Certificate of Citizenship
    - Census Records
- Cemetery
- Church
- City Directories
- Education
- Family Stories About Ancestor
- Funeral Home
- Land Grants / Deeds

- Migration
- Newspapers
- Obituary
- Occupation
- Photos
- Tax List
- Voter Lists
- Will / Probate
- _____
- _____
- _____
- _____
- _____

Ancestor's Name _____

Event	Month	Day	Year	Notes	Note #
Born					
Died					
Buried					
Father B.					
D.					
Mother B.					
D.					
Married 1					
Spouse 1 B.					
D.					
Married 2					
Spouse 2 B.					
D.					
Religion					
Occupation					
Military					
Residence					
Residence					

Children:

	Name	Date of Birth	Place of Birth	Death Date
1.				
2.				
3.				
4.				
5.				
6.				
7.				
8.				
9.				

Children continued:

	Name	Date of Birth	Place of Birth	Death Date
10.				
12.				
13.				
14.				
15.				
16.				
18.				
19.				
20.				

U.S. Federal Census

	State	County	Township	Notes
1790				
1800				
1810				
1820				
1830				
1840				
1850				
1860				
1870				
1880				
1890				
1900				
1910				
1920				
1930				

Notes/Source (Remember to number the note /source and link it to the above so you can find it faster.)

Chapter Two

When dealing with the census records keep in mind that they have evolved and changed over time. Some are quite basic in what information was recorded and others are more detailed. You can access the **1790** through **1940** census records as of now. The **1950** census should be available in 2022. The census records can be found at Historical Societies, National Archives, and even online at places like **www.ancestry.com, www.censusfinder.com**, and at **www.censuslinks.com,** as well as several other places. Some places are fee based while others can be accessed for free.

The first several census records **(1790-1810)** covered very basic information with the listing only of the head of house hold name and number of persons according to age groups and categories such as free white males and free white females.

It was in the **1820's to 1840's** that they added occupation, military pensions, students, and number of those not naturalized. By the **1850's** bigger changes occurred with the addition of having the name of everyone in the house hold, addresses, value of the estate if owned, and the place of birth. **1860** brought more information on slave ownership such as the name of the slave owner, number of slaves owned, and freed.

It was the **1870's** that added the important age of last birth date and month of birth for a child born with in the year. Also the fact that if the parents were foreign born was also added and the month of marriage if within the year was added also. The **1880's** brought us the important relationship to head of household and birth place of parents.

Now you need to be aware that there is a problem with the **1890** census. It was in 1921 that a fire caused a lot of damage to it. There are bits and pieces of it that may still be of use to you. If what you need was destroyed there are several special schedules for that year that you can look at. These are called union veterans and widows of union veterans. Tax lists may also be of some help for that year. It also gave to us the important year of immigration and asked if they were a survivor of the civil war. By the **1920** the census added the employer and number on the farm schedule and the **1930** census asked for marital status and age at the time of first marriage. The **1950** census will be released sometime in the year 2022.

Census records can be a great source of information and a conformation of an ancestor's residency and more but your ancestors can also be hard to find. There are ancestors that are not considered the head of house hold for various reasons. They are parents of the head of household, parents of his spouse, or some other relation. They maybe they are a boarder or live in employee. If they are hard to find keep these relationship possibilities in mind and you may find them after all.

Their last name could be misspelled because an enumerator could have misspelled the name due to the way the ancestor pronounced their name. Even if the enumerator got the spelling right their hand writing may not have been readable to the person who transcribed the census and the transcriber misspelled the name. Also over time writing can fade and make a letter **o** look like a letter **u.** In any case when searching the census records it's a good idea to keep in mind various ways a name could be spelled.

Another problem with names on census records and even in some other records is the name itself. There can be an issue of nicknames being used in census records such as using Bert instead of Robert that you need to be aware of. Then there are some ancestors that preferred to use their middle name instead of their first name for many reasons. One reason is to distinguish themselves from another family member with the same name, usually someone they are named after such as a parent or grandparent.

The age in the census records are based on how old your ancestors were on their last birthday. A problem with their age could occur for several different reasons. One reason for this is due to the date the census was taken in relationship to when a person had their birthday. The birthday may not have happened yet. Even if it was the next day they would have been listed as a year younger than what they would have been for the year the census was taken.

There are other reasons for a discrepancy to occur with the numbers. The enumerator could have written it down wrong due to a heavy accent the person had when talking to him. The person transcribing it may not have been able to read it correctly due to the handwriting being aged and faded. The hand writing may not be as legible as we would like and they put down what they thought it said. It's easy to mistake a 4 for a 9 if the top of the 9 was faded or a complete circle made at the top of the 9 was not made. There can also be a mistake made with the spellings of the names for some of these reasons as well.

So when looking at ages and names on the census records, keep it in mind that the age may very well be a little off and the names spelled a bit differently. It is always best to confirm the age and spelling of the names with other documents.

All in all the census records, even with some discrepancies, are worth researching and gathering information from. You will be able to use that information to find more about an ancestor and may even find other relatives as well. Pay attention to other people on the same page as well as at least one page a head or after the one you're ancestor is on. You could find other relatives that were living nearby.

Add any notes about the census records. Don't forget to add the ancestor's number at the beginning your notation.

Census Year _____   # Census Log   Page # _____

Family Name _____

#	Name	State	County	Township	Book #	Page #	Line #
1							
2							
3							
4							
5							
6							
7							
8							
9							
10							
11							
12							
13							
14							
15							
16							
17							
18							
19							
20							
21							
22							
23							
24							
25							
26							
27							
28							
29							
30							
31							
32							
33							
34							
35							

Add any notes about the census records. Don't forget to add the ancestor's number at the beginning your notation.

Census Year _____   # Census Log   Page # _____

Family Name _____

#	Name	State	County	Township	Book #	Page #	Line #
36							
37							
38							
39							
40							
41							
42							
43							
44							
45							
46							
47							
48							
49							
50							
51							
52							
53							
54							
55							
56							
57							
58							
59							
60							
61							
62							
63							
64							
65							
66							
67							
68							
69							
70							

Add any notes about the census records. Don't forget to add the ancestor's number at the beginning your notation.

Census Year_____ # Census Log Page # _____

Family Name_____

#	Name	State	County	Township	Book #	Page #	Line #
71							
72							
73							
74							
75							
76							
77							
78							
79							
80							
81							
82							
83							
84							
85							
86							
87							
88							
89							
90							
91							
92							
93							
94							
95							
96							
97							
98							
99							
100							
101							
102							
103							
104							
105							

Chapter Three

This section is be filled out by you in your search for cemeteries and funeral home information. You can take it with you when you are on a research trip or keep it beside you while you search the internet. You can keep track of the cemeteries and funeral homes that you want search for your ancestors. You will have them all in one place so you will always know which ones you have contacted and each ancestor you have found there. Also, you will have a record of the cemeteries and funeral homes you still need to contact.

You will find a cemetery research record where you will be able to add the following information for each ancestor: cemetery, section number, lot number, date of birth, and date of death. In the cemetery section you will have a space for you to add the directions to the cemeteries. These, worksheets when filled out, will help you to find your ancestors when you go to the cemeteries. You will have all the information with you that you need to find them. Just don't forget to add the cemetery section maps. You will be able to use it also for a quick search of your ancestors.

In the cemetery section you will find a place for the cemetery's name, location, address, and contact information. There is also a place for method of contact used, office hours, and directions to help you find it.

Once you have contacted the cemetery there is a space for you to document your findings about your ancestors as well as any funeral home information the cemetery may be able to provide. There is a place for you to add the section number of the cemetery your ancestor is buried in and the lot number. With these and a map of the cemetery you will be able to find your ancestor's headstone. There is also a space you can list other family members found buried nearby.

If you go to the cemetery or have the cemetery send you a photo of your ancestor's head stone you can add it here too or even a photo of the cemetery itself.

In the funeral home section you will find a place for the cemetery's name, location, address, and contact information. There is also a place for method of contact used, office hours, and directions to help you find it.

There is a space for your ancestor's name, birth, and death dates, conformation of funeral, date of burial, and family members associated with your ancestor. There is a place for you to check off if you find their death certificate, obituary, and any burial records. There is also a section for any cemetery information they may have available for you.

Cemetery

Cemetery Research can usually be done online and through county historical societies and libraries. One free online site I have found useful is Find A Grave. Some places have county cemetery indexes on computers in which you can search by your ancestor's last name faster and then go to the book indicated to get more information. You can of course contact different cemeteries near where your ancestors lived to find them as well as contacting funeral homes in the area.

Some cemetery record books that you may find not only give the dates on the head stone but the name of the cemetery and a map of the cemetery showing the section numbers. If you have the section numbers and the lot numbers you can go to the cemetery and find the grave site you're looking for with relative ease. If you can't find a map among the records you may want contact the cemetery's office itself to see if the cemetery has one. You should contact them any way to see what information you can gather from them on your ancestors.

Once you have arrived at the cemetery with the section and lot number of your ancestor, make sure you take the time to view the area and the placement of your ancestor's headstone with the others. Keeping an open mind to possibility that you may find relatives near the headstone of the ancestor you're looking for.

Many times, particularly in the past, you will find that families tended to bury family members not only in the same cemetery but together in the same section or side by side. Once you find a relative in one cemetery it is worth looking for more of his or her relatives there as well. So when you approach the section and lot of your ancestor make note of others buried there. You may find other relatives in the same section, next to or nearby. Also be sure to look on each side of the head stone as well. Sometimes another ancestor's information will be on your ancestor's head stone. I have an ancestor that was buried in a cemetery in Illinois but in Pennsylvania, on the headstone beside her husband's we found her name and information. On the other side of the stone with her information we found a man's information that had a different last name. We later found out he was her father.

If you find your ancestor among others that do not have the same last name do not discount them as relatives of your ancestor completely. A few headstones away from one of my ancestors we have a woman and her baby under yet a different name altogether who turned out to be a daughter of our ancestor. She had been married and had died young. You need to keep an open mind to possible relationships among the headstones because it can lead you to new information and just maybe you will breach a brick wall.

When you go to the cemetery and find the head stone you were looking for don't forget to take photos and write down all of the information you find on the head stone. Sometimes the inscription will be worn and hard to read. One way to help with this issue is to take at least two photos of the stone. One needs to be a close up photo of the headstone one so you can clearly see the inscription area and one at a bit of a distance away.

Some headstones cannot be read or are hard to read because of the wear and tear of time and any number of damages that could have occurred to the stone. A close up photo with the right photo computer program you may just be able to enhance the photo enough to make out what the head stone says. If you have a program that can make the photo look like a negative it may help in making the inscription readable.

Now don't get discouraged if even with a computer program you can't make out what it says. The office of the cemetery may also have it recorded in their records and you may be able to get a copy of it. There are other ways of finding the date of death or at least an approximant year of death as well. The church associated with the cemetery or a funeral home may have the information or information that could lead to finding the answer.

Cemeteries and funeral homes sometimes keep records beyond who and where they are buried. They can have family members associated with the lot, obituary, death certificate, and if the person buried there had been in the military. They may also be able to tell if family members are buried nearby. Though not all cemeteries and funeral homes will have a lot of detail about all who are buried there because of record loss or the date they started to keep records.

If you find they can't help you with the date on the head stone, you can't find an obituary and if the funeral home is not known or cannot help clear up the issue, there is one other option that could be of some help though it could take some researching. You may be able to narrow down the possible death date due to the kind of head stone is there.

The type of stone, the shape, and placement in the cemetery can sometimes to help with an approximant age of the stone and there for (a possible) approximant death dates if the stone is unreadable. I say possible because sometimes a family member will have taken note of the disrepair and unreadable inscription on the stone and replaced it with a newer one. In that case dating the head stone would not help with the death date but, it would leave another clue that may lead you to find more family members. The cemetery should have records about the replacement of a headstone and who had it placed there.

The photo of the stone from a little distance will give you an idea of the shape, and style of the head stone as well as the stones that are around it. You will be able to use this in comparing it to others of the time you believe your ancestor died. It is a good idea if you can determine what kind of stone it is made out of and any pictures, engravings, sculptures, or defining marks on the stone will be important too in dating a head stone if you need to.

Cemetery Research Record

Add Photo of the Cemetery or the Head Stone here

Cemetery Name_____
Location_____
Address_____
Phone Number_____
Email_____
Website_____

Method of contact used:

Phone__ on_____	**Hours:**	**Directions:**
Email___on_____		
Mail__on_____		
Visited___on_____		

Ancestor looking for; (additional Ancestors for this cemetery on back)
Name_____ Birth/Death Dates_____
Confirmation of Burial Y / N   Date of Burial_____ Section Number _____Lot #_____
    Copies of: Death Certificate_____ Obituary____ Burial Record____
    Family Members associated with the lot_____
_____

    Funeral Home used_____
    Address_____
    Phone Number_____
    Email_____
Other family members found buried nearby (Don't forget to add their dates)
_____
_____
_____

Ancestors Looking for;
Name_____ Birth/Death Dates_____
Confirmation of Burial Y / N   Date of Burial_____ Section Number _____Lot #_____
    Copies of: Death Certificate_____ Obituary____ Burial Record____
    Family Members associated with the lot_____
_____

    Funeral Home used_____
    Address_____
    Phone Number_____
    Email_____
Other family members found buried nearby (Don't forget to add their dates)
_____
_____

Ancestors Looking for;
Name_____ Birth/Death Dates_____
Confirmation of Burial Y / N   Date of Burial_____ Section Number _____Lot #_____
    Copies of: Death Certificate_____ Obituary_____ Burial Record____
    Family Members associated with the lot_____
    _____
    Funeral Home used_____
    Address_____
    Phone Number_____
    Email_____
Other family members found buried nearby (Don't forget to add their dates)
_____
_____

Ancestors Looking for;
Name_____ Birth/Death Dates_____
Confirmation of Burial Y / N   Date of Burial_____ Section Number _____Lot #_____
    Copies of: Death Certificate_____ Obituary_____ Burial Record____
    Family Members associated with the lot_____
    _____
    Funeral Home used_____
    Address_____
    Phone Number_____
    Email_____
Other family members found buried nearby (Don't forget to add their dates)
_____
_____

Ancestors Looking for;
Name_____ Birth/Death Dates_____
Confirmation of Burial Y / N   Date of Burial_____ Section Number _____Lot #_____
    Copies of: Death Certificate_____ Obituary_____ Burial Record____
    Family Members associated with the lot_____
    _____
    Funeral Home used_____
    Address_____
    Phone Number_____
    Email_____
Other family members found buried nearby (Don't forget to add their dates)
_____
_____

Cemetery Research Record

Add Photo of the Cemetery or the Head Stone here

Cemetery Name_____
Location_____
Address_____
Phone Number_____
Email_____
Website_____

Method of contact used:

Phone__ on_____	**Hours:**	**Directions:**
Email___on_____		
Mail__on_____		
Visited___on_____		

Ancestor looking for; (additional Ancestors for this cemetery on back)
Name_____ Birth/Death Dates_____
Confirmation of Burial Y / N   Date of Burial_____   Section Number _____ Lot #_____
    Copies of: Death Certificate_____ Obituary_____ Burial Record____
    Family Members associated with the lot_____
_____

    Funeral Home used_____
    Address_____
    Phone Number_____
    Email_____
Other family members found buried nearby (Don't forget to add their dates)
_____
_____
_____

Ancestors Looking for;
Name_____ Birth/Death Dates_____
Confirmation of Burial Y / N   Date of Burial_____   Section Number _____ Lot #_____
    Copies of: Death Certificate_____ Obituary_____ Burial Record____
    Family Members associated with the lot_____
_____

    Funeral Home used_____
    Address_____
    Phone Number_____
    Email_____
Other family members found buried nearby (Don't forget to add their dates)
_____
_____

Ancestors Looking for;
Name_____ Birth/Death Dates_____
Confirmation of Burial Y / N   Date of Burial_____   Section Number _____Lot #_____
    Copies of: Death Certificate_____ Obituary____ Burial Record____
    Family Members associated with the lot_____
    _____
    Funeral Home used_____
    Address_____
    Phone Number_____
    Email_____
Other family members found buried nearby (Don't forget to add their dates)
_____
_____

Ancestors Looking for;
Name_____ Birth/Death Dates_____
Confirmation of Burial Y / N   Date of Burial_____   Section Number _____Lot #_____
    Copies of: Death Certificate_____ Obituary____ Burial Record____
    Family Members associated with the lot_____
    _____
    Funeral Home used_____
    Address_____
    Phone Number_____
    Email_____
Other family members found buried nearby (Don't forget to add their dates)
_____
_____

Ancestors Looking for;
Name_____ Birth/Death Dates_____
Confirmation of Burial Y / N   Date of Burial_____   Section Number _____Lot #_____
    Copies of: Death Certificate_____ Obituary____ Burial Record____
    Family Members associated with the lot_____
    _____
    Funeral Home used_____
    Address_____
    Phone Number_____
    Email_____
Other family members found buried nearby (Don't forget to add their dates)
_____
_____

Cemetery Research Record

> Add Photo of the Cemetery or the Head Stone here

Cemetery Name_____
Location_____
Address_____
Phone Number_____
Email_____
Website_____

Method of contact used:

Phone__ on_____	**Hours:**	**Directions:**
Email___on_____		
Mail__on_____		
Visited___on_____		

Ancestor looking for; (additional Ancestors for this cemetery on back)
Name_____ Birth/Death Dates_____
Confirmation of Burial Y / N   Date of Burial_____   Section Number _____Lot #_____
    Copies of: Death Certificate_____ Obituary_____ Burial Record____
    Family Members associated with the lot_____
_____

    Funeral Home used_____
    Address_____
    Phone Number_____
    Email_____
Other family members found buried nearby (Don't forget to add their dates)
_____
_____
_____

Ancestors Looking for;
Name_____ Birth/Death Dates_____
Confirmation of Burial Y / N   Date of Burial_____   Section Number _____Lot #_____
    Copies of: Death Certificate_____ Obituary_____ Burial Record____
    Family Members associated with the lot_____
_____

    Funeral Home used_____
    Address_____
    Phone Number_____
    Email_____
Other family members found buried nearby (Don't forget to add their dates)
_____
_____

Ancestors Looking for;
Name_____ Birth/Death Dates_____
Confirmation of Burial Y / N   Date of Burial_____ Section Number _____ Lot #_____
    Copies of: Death Certificate_____ Obituary____ Burial Record____
    Family Members associated with the lot_____
    _____
    Funeral Home used_____
    Address_____
    Phone Number_____
    Email_____
Other Family members found buried nearby (Don't forget to add their dates)
_____
_____

Ancestors Looking for;
Name_____ Birth/Death Dates_____
Confirmation of Burial Y / N   Date of Burial_____ Section Number _____ Lot #_____
    Copies of: Death Certificate_____ Obituary____ Burial Record____
    Family Members associated with the lot_____
    _____
    Funeral Home used_____
    Address_____
    Phone Number_____
    Email_____
Other Family members found buried nearby (Don't forget to add their dates)
_____
_____

Ancestors Looking for;
Name_____ Birth/Death Dates_____
Confirmation of Burial Y / N   Date of Burial_____ Section Number _____ Lot #_____
    Copies of: Death Certificate_____ Obituary____ Burial Record____
    Family Members associated with the lot_____
    _____
    Funeral Home used_____
    Address_____
    Phone Number_____
    Email_____
Other Family members found buried nearby (Don't forget to add their dates)

Cemetery Research Record

Add Photo of the Cemetery or the Head Stone here

Cemetery Name_____
Location_____
Address_____
Phone Number_____
Email_____
Website_____

Method of contact used:

Phone__ on_____ Email___on_____ Mail__on_____ Visited___on_____	**Hours:**	**Directions:**

Ancestor looking for; (additional Ancestors for this cemetery on back)
Name_____ Birth/Death Dates_____
Confirmation of Burial Y / N   Date of Burial_____ Section Number _____ Lot #_____
    Copies of: Death Certificate_____ Obituary_____ Burial Record____
    Family Members associated with the lot_____
_____

    Funeral Home used_____
    Address_____
    Phone Number_____
    Email_____
Other family members found buried nearby (Don't forget to add their dates)
_____
_____
_____

Ancestors Looking for;
Name_____ Birth/Death Dates_____
Confirmation of Burial Y / N   Date of Burial_____ Section Number _____ Lot #_____
    Copies of: Death Certificate_____ Obituary_____ Burial Record____
    Family Members associated with the lot_____
_____

    Funeral Home used_____
    Address_____
    Phone Number_____
    Email_____
Other family members found buried nearby (Don't forget to add their dates)
_____
_____

Ancestors Looking for;
Name_____ Birth/Death Dates_____
Confirmation of Burial Y / N   Date of Burial_____   Section Number _____Lot #_____
    Copies of: Death Certificate_____ Obituary_____ Burial Record_____
    Family Members associated with the lot_____
    _____
    Funeral Home used_____
    Address_____
    Phone Number_____
    Email_____
Other family members found buried nearby (Don't forget to add their dates)
_____
_____

Ancestors Looking for;
Name_____ Birth/Death Dates_____
Confirmation of Burial Y / N   Date of Burial_____   Section Number _____Lot #_____
    Copies of: Death Certificate_____ Obituary_____ Burial Record_____
    Family Members associated with the lot_____
    _____
    Funeral Home used_____
    Address_____
    Phone Number_____
    Email_____
Other family members found buried nearby (Don't forget to add their dates)
_____
_____

Ancestors Looking for;
Name_____ Birth/Death Dates_____
Confirmation of Burial Y / N   Date of Burial_____   Section Number _____Lot #_____
    Copies of: Death Certificate_____ Obituary_____ Burial Record_____
    Family Members associated with the lot_____
    _____
    Funeral Home used_____
    Address_____
    Phone Number_____
    Email_____
Other family members found buried nearby (Don't forget to add their dates)
_____
_____

Funeral Home Records

Funeral home records can be quite helpful. They sometimes can provide copies of death certificates, obituaries, and know what newspaper the obituaries were put into.

They should have information on the families attached to the ancestor you're looking for. For example, name of the family member who was in charge of planning the funeral and burial. They also may know what the relationship between that person and your ancestor was. There could also be information associated with other family members as well.

The funeral home would know where the burial had taken place and perhaps the date and time of death, where your ancestor died and may even have the date of birth.

If your ancestor was involved in the military, the funeral home and cemetery should have a record of that as well. They may have had a military honors funeral service which may give you details of his or her military career. Many times you will find a military marker beside the head stone. There are times that even though they were in the military a marker may not be beside the head stone for various reasons. You may be able to look into having one placed there if you can prove their military service.

The religion of your ancestor may also be discovered through the funeral home. If a religious service was preformed there or at the cemetery you may be able to find out what religion they were and church they attended. This could lead to church records and more family information. It is always a good idea to try and find the funeral home, cemetery, and even the church that an ancestor is associated with.

With the internet these places may very well be found with a bit of researching. You may want to talk to older family members who may be able to tell you which funeral homes and cemeteries are generally used by the family. Though same ones are typically used out of tradition with in a family it is a good idea not to discount others.

Funeral Home Information List

Funeral Home Name_____
Location_____
Address_____
Phone Number_____
Email_____
Website_____
Method of Contact Used:

Notes:

Phone__ on_____ Email___on_____ Mail__on_____ Visited___on_____	**Hours:**	**Directions:**

Ancestor looking for: (additional Ancestors for this cemetery on back)
Name_____ Birth/Death Dates_____
Confirmation of Funeral Y / N   Date of Funeral_____   Date of Burial_____
    Copies of: Death Certificate_____   Obituary_____   Burial Record_____
    Family Members associated with the Funeral_____
    _____

    Cemetery used_____
    Address_____
    Phone Number_____
    Email_____
Notes_____
_____
_____
_____
_____
_____

Ancestor looking for:
Name_____ Birth/Death Dates_____
Confirmation of Funeral Y / N   Date of Funeral_____   Date of Burial_____
    Copies of: Death Certificate_____   Obituary_____   Burial Record_____
    Family Members associated with the Funeral_____
    _____

    Cemetery used_____
    Address_____
    Phone Number_____
    Email_____
Notes_____
_____
_____

Ancestor looking for:
Name_____ Birth/Death Dates_____
Confirmation of Funeral Y / N   Date of Funeral_____ Date of Burial_____
    Copies of: Death Certificate_____ Obituary_____ Burial Record____
    Family Members associated with the Funeral_____
_____

    Cemetery used_____
    Address_____
    Phone Number_____
    Email_____
Notes_____
_____
_____
_____

Ancestor looking for:
Name_____ Birth/Death Dates_____
Confirmation of Funeral Y / N   Date of Funeral_____ Date of Burial_____
    Copies of: Death Certificate_____ Obituary_____ Burial Record____
    Family Members associated with the Funeral_____
_____

    Cemetery used_____
    Address_____
    Phone Number_____
    Email_____
Notes_____
_____
_____
_____

Ancestor looking for:
Name_____ Birth/Death Dates_____
Confirmation of Funeral Y / N   Date of Funeral_____ Date of Burial_____
    Copies of: Death Certificate_____ Obituary_____ Burial Record____
    Family Members associated with the Funeral_____
_____

    Cemetery used_____
    Address_____
    Phone Number_____
    Email_____
Notes_____
_____
_____
_____

Funeral Home Information List

Funeral Home Name_____
Location_____
Address_____
Phone Number_____
Email_____
Website_____

Method of Contact Used:

Notes:

Phone__ on_____ Email___on_____ Mail__on_____ Visited___on_____	**Hours:**	**Directions:**

Ancestor looking for: (additional Ancestors for this cemetery on back)
Name_____ Birth/Death Dates_____
Confirmation of Funeral Y / N   Date of Funeral_____ Date of Burial_____
    Copies of: Death Certificate_____   Obituary_____   Burial Record____
    Family Members associated with the Funeral_____

    Cemetery used_____
    Address_____
    Phone Number_____
    Email_____
Notes_____
_____
_____
_____
_____

Ancestor looking for:
Name_____ Birth/Death Dates_____
Confirmation of Funeral Y / N   Date of Funeral_____ Date of Burial_____
    Copies of: Death Certificate_____   Obituary_____   Burial Record____
    Family Members associated with the Funeral_____

    Cemetery used_____
    Address_____
    Phone Number_____
    Email_____
Notes_____
_____
_____

Ancestor looking for:
Name_____ Birth/Death Dates_____
Confirmation of Funeral Y / N   Date of Funeral_____   Date of Burial_____
    Copies of: Death Certificate_____ Obituary_____ Burial Record____
    Family Members associated with the Funeral_____
    _____
    Cemetery used_____
    Address_____
    Phone Number_____
    Email_____
Notes_____
_____
_____
_____

Ancestor looking for:
Name_____ Birth/Death Dates_____
Confirmation of Funeral Y / N   Date of Funeral_____   Date of Burial_____
    Copies of: Death Certificate_____ Obituary_____ Burial Record____
    Family Members associated with the Funeral_____
    _____
    Cemetery used_____
    Address_____
    Phone Number_____
    Email_____
Notes_____
_____
_____
_____

Ancestor looking for:
Name_____ Birth/Death Dates_____
Confirmation of Funeral Y / N   Date of Funeral_____   Date of Burial_____
    Copies of: Death Certificate_____ Obituary_____ Burial Record____
    Family Members associated with the Funeral_____
    _____
    Cemetery used_____
    Address_____
    Phone Number_____
    Email_____
Notes_____
_____
_____
_____

Funeral Home Information List

Funeral Home Name_____
Location_____
Address_____
Phone Number_____
Email_____
Website_____

Notes:

Method of Contact Used:

Phone__ on_____	**Hours:**	**Directions:**
Email___on_____		
Mail__on_____		
Visited___on_____		

Ancestor looking for: (additional Ancestors for this cemetery on back)
Name_____ Birth/Death Dates_____
Confirmation of Funeral Y / N   Date of Funeral_____ Date of Burial_____
    Copies of: Death Certificate_____ Obituary_____ Burial Record_____
    Family Members associated with the Funeral_____
_____
    Cemetery used_____
    Address_____
    Phone Number_____
    Email_____
Notes_____
_____
_____
_____
_____
_____

Ancestor looking for:
Name_____ Birth/Death Dates_____
Confirmation of Funeral Y / N   Date of Funeral_____ Date of Burial_____
    Copies of: Death Certificate_____ Obituary_____ Burial Record_____
    Family Members associated with the Funeral_____
_____
    Cemetery used_____
    Address_____
    Phone Number_____
    Email_____
Notes_____
_____
_____

Ancestor looking for:
Name_____ Birth/Death Dates_____
Confirmation of Funeral Y / N   Date of Funeral_____   Date of Burial_____
    Copies of: Death Certificate_____   Obituary_____   Burial Record____
    Family Members associated with the Funeral_____
    _____
    Cemetery used_____
    Address_____
    Phone Number_____
    Email_____
Notes_____
_____
_____
_____

Ancestor looking for:
Name_____ Birth/Death Dates_____
Confirmation of Funeral Y / N   Date of Funeral_____   Date of Burial_____
    Copies of: Death Certificate_____   Obituary_____   Burial Record____
    Family Members associated with the Funeral_____
    _____
    Cemetery used_____
    Address_____
    Phone Number_____
    Email_____
Notes_____
_____
_____
_____

Ancestor looking for:
Name_____ Birth/Death Dates_____
Confirmation of Funeral Y / N   Date of Funeral_____   Date of Burial_____
    Copies of: Death Certificate_____   Obituary_____   Burial Record____
    Family Members associated with the Funeral_____
    _____
    Cemetery used_____
    Address_____
    Phone Number_____
    Email_____
Notes_____
_____
_____
_____

Funeral Home Information List

Funeral Home Name_____
Location_____
Address_____
Phone Number_____
Email_____
Website_____

Notes:

Method of Contact Used:

Phone__ on_____ Email___on_____ Mail__on_____ Visited___on_____	**Hours:**	**Directions:**

Ancestor looking for: (additional Ancestors for this cemetery on back)
Name_____ Birth/Death Dates_____
Confirmation of Funeral Y / N   Date of Funeral_____ Date of Burial_____
    Copies of: Death Certificate_____ Obituary_____ Burial Record_____
    Family Members associated with the Funeral_____

    Cemetery used_____
    Address_____
    Phone Number_____
    Email_____
Notes_____
_____
_____
_____
_____

Ancestor looking for:
Name_____ Birth/Death Dates_____
Confirmation of Funeral Y / N   Date of Funeral_____ Date of Burial_____
    Copies of: Death Certificate_____ Obituary_____ Burial Record_____
    Family Members associated with the Funeral_____

    Cemetery used_____
    Address_____
    Phone Number_____
    Email_____
Notes_____
_____
_____

Ancestor looking for:
Name_____ Birth/Death Dates_____
Confirmation of Funeral Y / N   Date of Funeral_____ Date of Burial_____
    Copies of: Death Certificate_____ Obituary_____ Burial Record____
    Family Members associated with the Funeral_____
_____

    Cemetery used_____
    Address_____
    PhoneNumber_____
    Email_____
Notes_____
_____
_____
_____

Ancestor looking for:
Name_____ Birth/Death Dates_____
Confirmation of Funeral Y / N   Date of Funeral_____ Date of Burial_____
    Copies of: Death Certificate_____ Obituary_____ Burial Record____
    Family Members associated with the Funeral_____
_____

    Cemetery used_____
    Address_____
    Phone Number_____
    Email_____
Notes_____
_____
_____
_____

Ancestor looking for:
Name_____ Birth/Death Dates_____
Confirmation of Funeral Y / N   Date of Funeral_____ Date of Burial_____
    Copies of: Death Certificate_____ Obituary_____ Burial Record____
    Family Members associated with the Funeral_____
_____

    Cemetery used_____
    Address_____
    Phone Number_____
    Email_____
Notes_____
_____
_____
_____

Chapter Four

The County Court House Records

The research worksheets will help you with your research and listing where you found the records. This is so you can go back to view the records again or to note as an informational source. Take this book with you when you go to a county court house to search for these records and record your findings in it.

The county court house records can be a great source of information for genealogists. Some of the records that can be found at county court houses are birth, marriage, deeds, death, and naturalization records. The information in these records will contain names and dates for these events but they can also give you other family members and information as well.

The date at which each county court house started recording these events will vary from county to county. Also keep in mind that as with townships, counties were created from other larger counties or regions. Records did not always change hands when this would happen. So you may need to check the dates that these changes occurred or when they started keeping these records. You may just find out that the records you are looking for are in another county.

Another reason for not finding records where you think they should be can be due to the fact that they could have been destroyed in a fire or flood. Whatever the reason you still may be able to find the information you need through historical societies, churches, cemeteries, and funeral homes to name a few. All in all these records are usually a great source of dates and information on your ancestors that makes them well worth looking into.

Birth Research Log/Record

Birth records usually will tell you where, when and to whom a child was born. The Birth Record Log in this book is to help you at the court house when searching the birth records. It will help keep track of those you have found and those you still want to look for. It also will help you keep track of which county and state you have looked for your ancestors. You can use these pages one page per surname if you wish.

The Birth Research Log/Record has a place for the first and last name of the ancestor you are looking for. There is also place for you to put the court house's book number that you will find the certificate information in as well as the page/certificate number for the birth record. The parents and birth date also has a space for each ancestor. If you already know this information this will help confirm that you have the right record. If not than you will be able to fill it in as you find the records.

May times there will be an index that will tell you which record book and page/certificate number to find the record in. This log will aid you in collecting the information on each individual you are looking for as you search the index. Once the log is competed it will also give you a list of sources to use for verifying the records you have found. If you run out of time at the court house and need to go back at a later date to find look at the certificates in the books you will not have to go through the index again. You will have all the information you will need already.

Getting a photo copy of the record often comes in handy and saves time at the court house. If for some reason you can't get a photo copy of the record you may be allowed to take a photo of it. This way if any questions come up on the notes you took you will not have to go back to the court house again to look at it.

Birth Record

County of _____ State of _____

Last Name of Family _____

Last Name	First Name	Book #	Page or Certificate #	Mother	Father	Date

Birth Record

County of _____ State of _____

Last Name of Family _____

Last Name	First Name	Book #	Page or Certificate #	Mother	Father	Date

Marriage Record

The basic information you will find here is the bride's name, the groom's name, their age, and occupation. There should also be the name of the person who performed the marriage and even some times where the marriage took place in that county, as well as the occupations of the bride, and groom. If either the bride or groom were under age at the time of the marriage then a separate document would be attached the marriage record singed by a parent or next of kin to give consent to the marriage.

The marriage record log in this book will help you at the court house when searching the marriage records. It will help keep track of those you have found and those you still want to look for. It also will help you keep track of which county and state you have looked at for your ancestors. You can use these pages one page per surname if you wish. It has a place for the name of the bride and groom, and the marriage date.

The court house's book number and certificate number space will help you find the certificate information in as well as the page/certificate number for the marriage record. If you already know this information this will help confirm that you have the right record. If not, then you will be able to fill it in as you find the records.

May times there will be an index that will tell you which record book and page/certificate number to find the record in. This log will aid you in collecting the information on each individual you are looking for as you search the index. Once the log is competed it will also give you a list of sources to use for verifying the records you have found. If you run out of time at the court house and need to go back at a later date to find look at the certificates in the books you will not have to go through the index again. You will have all the information you will need already.

Getting a photo copy of the record often comes in handy and saves time at the court house. If for some reason you can't get a photo copy of the record you may be allowed to take a photo of it. This way if any questions come up on the notes you took you will not have to go back to the court house again to look at it.

Marriage Records

County of _____ State of _____
Last Name of Family_____

Bride	Groom	Date	Book #	Certificate #

Marriage Records

County of _____ State of _____
Last Name of Family _____

Bride	Groom	Date	Book #	Certificate #

Death Records

Death records may reveal next of kin, when and where they were born. They may also give if they were married and what occupation they had. It's possible that if they were in the military that too may be on recorded. Of course cause of death should be there as well, which would aid in starting a family medical history. Sometimes a last will and testament is available. This will give more information on family names and relationships.

The Death research log in this book will help you at the court house when searching for the death records. It will help keep track of those you have found and those you still want to look for. It also will help you keep track of which county and state you have looked in for your ancestors. You can use these pages one page per surname if you wish.

The court house's book number and certificate number space will help you find the certificate information in as well as the page/certificate number for the death record. If you already know this information this will help confirm that you have the right record. If not then you will be able to fill it in as you find the records.

There may be an index that will tell you which record book and page/certificate number to find the record in. Once the log is competed it will also give you a list of sources to use for verifying the records you have found. If you run out of time at the court house and need to go back at a later date to look at the certificates in the books you will not have to go through the index again. You will have all the information you will need already.

Getting a photo copy of the record often comes in handy and saves time at the court house. If for some reason you can't get a photo copy of the record you may be allowed to take a photo of it. This way if any questions come up on the notes you took you will not have to go back to the court house again to look at it.

Death Research Log

County of _____ State of _____
Family of _____

Name	Date of Death	Certificate #	Book #	Page #	Place of Death	Notes

Death Research Log

County of _____ State of _____
Family of _____

Name	Date of Death	Certificate #	Book #	Page #	Place of Death	Notes

Naturalization

As far as the naturalization records go they can be a bit tricky to find them all. A person coming to America wanting to become naturalized had several steps to go through before it became finalized.

The naturalization process changed over time and depending on the year you are searching you will need to be aware of the rules. There were a minimum number of years an immigrant had to have been in America and a minimum number of years they had to have lived in the state where they wanted to start the process before they could. Then after the intent to become naturalized had been filed there was another wait until they could file naturalization papers. During this time period they could move to another state and file the final naturalization papers there. They also had to have references from someone who was already a citizen.

Now citizenship for children and the wives were in connection with that of the husband/father for some time. The fact that a child born in America did not always mean that they were considered as being a citizen upon birth, even if the parents were not. That came into law eventually but keep in mind it was not always so. If a child was under a certain age when their father became a citizen then they too gained citizenship. If not then they had to go through the process as well if they were to be considered a citizen.

If you know the date of naturalization or approximant year you can search the internet for the requirements for citizenship for that time period. It helps knowing this information because it could very well tell you what year your ancestor immigrated and just how long he resided in a particular state and where to look for the records.

The Naturalization Research Log in this book will help you at the court house when searching for the naturalization records. It will help keep track of those you have found and those you still want to look for. It also will help you keep track of which county and state you have looked in for your ancestors. You can use these pages one page per surname if you wish. Once, competed it will also give you a list of sources to use for verifying the records you have found. I have included a section as well for the recording of naturalization information that could be found on a Naturalization Petition

Getting a photo copy of the record often comes in handy and saves time at the court house. If for some reason you can't get a photo copy of the record you may be allowed to take a photo of it. This way if any questions come up on the notes you took you will not have to go back to the court house again to look at it again.

Naturalization Research Records

County of _____ State of _____

Location of Record Found _____

If you already know this information this will help confirm that you have the right record. If not then you will be able to fill it in as you find the records.

Full Name	
Date of Birth	Place of Birth
Occupation	

Current Residence at time of petition _____

Wife's Name		Birthdate	
Child's Name		Birthdate	
Child's Name		Birthdate	
Child's Name		Birthdate	
Child's Name		Birthdate	
Child's Name		Birthdate	
Child's Name		Birthdate	

Date of Petition	District Court	Emigration Date	Emigration from	Date of Emigration

Port of Arrival	Date of Arrival	Name of Vessel

Witnesses _____

Notes:

Naturalization Research Records

County of _____ State of_____

Location of Record Found_____

_____

If you already know this information this will help confirm that you have the right record. If not then you will be able to fill it in as you find the records.

Full Name	
Date of Birth	Place of Birth
Occupation	

Current Residence at time of petition_____

Wife's Name		Birthdate	
Child's Name		Birthdate	
Child's Name		Birthdate	
Child's Name		Birthdate	
Child's Name		Birthdate	
Child's Name		Birthdate	
Child's Name		Birthdate	

Date of Petition	District Court	Emigration Date	Emigration from	Date of Emigration

Port of Arrival	Date of Arrival	Name of Vessel

Witnesses_____

_____

_____

Notes:

Naturalization Research Records

County of _____ State of _____

Location of Record Found _____
_____

If you already know this information this will help confirm that you have the right record. If not then you will be able to fill it in as you find the records.

Full Name	
Date of Birth	Place of Birth
Occupation	

Current Residence at time of petition _____

Wife's Name		Birthdate	
Child's Name		Birthdate	
Child's Name		Birthdate	
Child's Name		Birthdate	
Child's Name		Birthdate	
Child's Name		Birthdate	
Child's Name		Birthdate	

Date of Petition	District Court	Emigration Date	Emigration from	Date of Emigration

Port of Arrival	Date of Arrival	Name of Vessel

Witnesses _____
_____
_____

Notes:

Naturalization Research Records

County of _____ State of _____
Location of Record Found _____
_____

If you already know this information this will help confirm that you have the right record. If not then you will be able to fill it in as you find the records.

Full Name	
Date of Birth	Place of Birth
Occupation	

Current Residence at time of petition _____

Wife's Name		Birthdate	
Child's Name		Birthdate	
Child's Name		Birthdate	
Child's Name		Birthdate	
Child's Name		Birthdate	
Child's Name		Birthdate	
Child's Name		Birthdate	

Date of Petition	District Court	Emigration Date	Emigration from	Date of Emigration

Port of Arrival	Date of Arrival	Name of Vessel

Witnesses _____
_____
_____

Notes:

Land/Deeds

The land/deed research log in this book will help you at the court house when searching for the land records. It will help keep track of those you have found and those you still want to look for. It also will help you keep track of which county and state you have searched land/deed records for your ancestors. You can use these pages one page per surname if you wish.

The indexes for the land/deed records are most likely are listed under the grantor or grantee's names. The term grantor means the person who is selling the land. The grantee is the person buying the land. You will then have to search them page by page to find your ancestor. You can put the ancestor's name you want to look for in the right column before you go to the court house and then you will have every one you want to search for on hand. I advise putting the names in alphabetical order to make searching easier. You will be able to fill the rest of this information in as you find the records.

Once the log is competed it will also give you a list of sources to use for verifying the records you have found. If you run out of time at the court house and need to go back at a later date to find look at the land/deed records you will have all the information you will need already to locate them.

Land /deed records can be useful in searching for information on your ancestors but don't be surprised if you don't always find land records for some. As with today, some of our ancestors did not always own the land they lived on. Some rented land and homes, some were borders and then there were the ancestors who were employees of the people who owned the land. Searching for land/deeds is still worth doing because of the potential information that you may gain.

One piece of information that you will be able find is the date they bought the land. Keep in mind that the date may not be the exact date they moved on to the land. It dose though give you an approximant date that they came to that county. If they were coming from far away the husband of a family would sometimes come by himself to check out the area and buy some land for his family and at a later date they would move there. Sometimes the delay in moving on to the land was because they needed to save up some more money to travel to the newly acquired land and build a home.

The land records usually give the place where they lived at the time they bought the land. This will help document their residency there and possibly give you clues as to where to look for them next. It is always a good idea to check the land records where they had been living at the time of the sale to see if they owned land before. It will give you an idea where they lived before that as well. It establishes a trail for you to follow. Keep in mind that just because they left one place to move somewhere else does not mean they didn't move back to the same area that they left so it makes sense to look completely through the land/deed records and not stop when you find one record.

Another thing to keep in mind is that just because they moved on to a different place does not mean they sold the land they left before they moved. They may have given it to someone else even. It is also possible that they sold it later after the move. It then stands to reason that it is a good idea to search for the sale of this land as well as when they bought it you just may find a connection.

You can learn how much land they owned and where it's located or a brief description of it. Farmers sometimes would also buy more land around or nearby later on in order to expand the farm. Sometimes their grown children would buy land adjacent to or nearby their parents to raise their own family and farm for themselves. The grown children may even add their land to their parents and thus continue to farm with their parents while expanding the family farm.

The land records will also tell you who sold them the land. Don't be surprised to find a parent or relative either sold or gifted them with land. This could be useful for you as well. It will include the price they paid for the land, if it was not a gift, and how many acres were sold.

One of your ancestors, if they had been in the military during the Revolutionary War or the War of 1812 very well could have received land for their service as a form of payment. In this situation you may find more information about him. You may find not only his residence but information on his enlistment. The information could be as simple as which company or regiment he was in to how long he was enlisted and his rank. If he actually moved on to that land it could be the reason he moved. He may have sold the land or gifted it to someone, just because he bounty land does not necessarily mean he kept it or lived on it.

Over all, land and deeds can be a good source of information and proof of residency. They can lead you on your search back to other places your ancestors lived and may give a clue to what kind of life they lived, were they farmers, store owners, or had some other type of occupation? Did they live in a small town, city or did they live in the country?

Land/Deed Log

County of _____ State of _____

Last Name of Family _____

Grantor	Grantee	Book#	Page #	Date

Land/Deed Log

County of _____ State of _____

Last Name of Family _____

Grantor	Grantee	Book#	Page #	Date

Chapter 5

Military Records

Information on an ancestor's military record can be very helpful in gathering facts on not only that particular ancestor but also about his family as well. If you can gather enough facts on his military service you may be able to obtain his service record from the United States National Archives. You may also learn enough to trace his movements throughout the war, any wounds, or mishaps he may have encountered on the way. If he was involved in any of the wars major battles you may even be able to trace his movements during them as well. The major battle fields in America like Gettysburg may very well have information on your ancestor, monuments to his regiment, and company with his name listed.

The United States National Archives has service records from the Revolutionary War through World War 2 that you may be able to order for a fee. Now from World War 2 forward, you either need to be the service man or woman or the next of kin to obtain information on them. Though, going backwards you should be able to order the records. You will need to fill out a form either on line or through the mail to request the information and pay a fee. The more information that you have on your ancestor the more likely the National Archives will be able to find the records you are looking for. The service records can sometimes be quite detailed from what dates they enrolled or were drafted and date of discharge to the wounds they received, battles they were in, and more. You may be able to get pension records for them as well. Pension records will give you information on them and their families after the war such as residence, occupation, members of the family, dates and possibly their health.

When researching for military information the first place to head would be to talk to relatives to see if they know any information about the military service in the family. Then using the internet search engines can be of help by putting in the ancestor's name and some of the information you have gathered. For example, when I put James L. Griffin Civil War Pennsylvania into a search engine, this is one of several sites that was the result: 140th Pennsylvania Infantry Soldier Roster - Civil War Index www.civilwarindex.com/armypa/.../140th_pa_infantry_roster.pdf. The more or different combinations of information you put into the search engine you may be lucky enough to get a lot of results.

There are many internet sites devoted to the wars. Some of the regiments and companies from the wars have their own sites. Historical societies, libraries, and state and county history books sometimes will have military rosters you can look through and information on the various wars.

The following Military Log will help you gather the information you will need to order or find the military record on your ancestor. Fill in the appropriate spaces and before you know it you will have all the information you need to trace them through their military service.

Ancestor's Name	
War	
Rank	
Company	
Regiment	
Date of Enlistment	
Date of Discharge	
Pension	
Disability	

Ancestor's Name	
War	
Rank	
Company	
Regiment	
Date of Enlistment	
Date of Discharge	
Pension	
Disability	

Ancestor's Name	
War	
Rank	
Company	
Regiment	
Date of Enlistment	
Date of Discharge	
Pension	
Disability	

Ancestor's Name	
War	
Rank	
Company	
Regiment	
Date of Enlistment	
Date of Discharge	
Pension	
Disability	

Ancestor's Name	
War	
Rank	
Company	
Regiment	
Date of Enlistment	
Date of Discharge	
Pension	
Disability	

Ancestor's Name	
War	
Rank	
Company	
Regiment	
Date of Enlistment	
Date of Discharge	
Pension	
Disability	

Ancestor's Name	
War	
Rank	
Company	
Regiment	
Date of Enlistment	
Date of Discharge	
Pension	
Disability	

Ancestor's Name	
War	
Rank	
Company	
Regiment	
Date of Enlistment	
Date of Discharge	
Pension	
Disability	

Ancestor's Name	
War	
Rank	
Company	
Regiment	
Date of Enlistment	
Date of Discharge	
Pension	
Disability	

Ancestor's Name	
War	
Rank	
Company	
Regiment	
Date of Enlistment	
Date of Discharge	
Pension	
Disability	

Ancestor's Name	
War	
Rank	
Company	
Regiment	
Date of Enlistment	
Date of Discharge	
Pension	
Disability	

Ancestor's Name	
War	
Rank	
Company	
Regiment	
Date of Enlistment	
Date of Discharge	
Pension	
Disability	

Ancestor's Name	
War	
Rank	
Company	
Regiment	
Date of Enlistment	
Date of Discharge	
Pension	
Disability	

Ancestor's Name	
War	
Rank	
Company	
Regiment	
Date of Enlistment	
Date of Discharge	
Pension	
Disability	

Ancestor's Name	
War	
Rank	
Company	
Regiment	
Date of Enlistment	
Date of Discharge	
Pension	
Disability	

Ancestor's Name	
War	
Rank	
Company	
Regiment	
Date of Enlistment	
Date of Discharge	
Pension	
Disability	

Chapter 6

Library Research

Libraries can be a great place to research your family tree. There are some libraries that have sections devoted to special collections and /or genealogy research. Even small community libraries can be very helpful. Libraries usually carry history books for the county they reside in and perhaps other counties close by. They usually have state histories as well. With inter library loan programs you may also be able to read books from other libraries you would not normally be able to travel to and read.

It is always a good idea to visit or contact the libraries that are close to where your ancestors lived when doing genealogy research. The librarians may be able to help you with the library research and possibly point you in a direction you had not thought of.

It is a good idea to keep track of the reference books and special collections the libraries have that may be of some help to you, as well as the books you are able to check out and take home to read. You may want to go back to them either for more information or to verify something. You may also want to use the information to help with citing the source of your information.

Library Research Lists

Library_____ Address_____
Phone_____ Web Site_____

Reference Books and Special Collections List

Call Number	Title	Author	Notes

Library Research Lists

Library_____ Address_____
Phone_____ Web Site_____

Reference Books and Special Collections List

Call Number	Title	Author	Notes

Library Research Lists

Library_____ Address_____
Phone_____ Web Site_____

Reference Books and Special Collections List

Call Number	Title	Author	Notes

Library Research Lists

Library_____ Address_____
Phone_____ Web Site_____

Reference Books and Special Collections List

Call Number	Title	Author	Notes

Library Research Lists

Books to Check Out

Call Number	Title	Author	Notes

Books to Check Out

Call Number	Title	Author	Notes

Books to Check Out

Call Number	Title	Author	Notes

Web Sites

In This chapter you will be able to keep track of the many web sites that you use in your family tree research. In the Web Log you have a place to write in the web address, the names of the ancestors you want to use the web site for, your ancestor's birth date, death date, and spouse's name. These facts will help you in searching the web site. It will help you to keep track of the ancestors you looked for or still need to look on for these sites.

The Web Accounts page is to help you keep track of the web sites that you have accounts with or need to log on to in order to use. It has a place for you to write down the web site, your user name, password, and the dollar amount ($) you are charged to use the site if any. It also has a place for you to write down if it is a daily, monthly, or yearly payment, the date you started the account, and the date you ended the account. The dates will help you keep track of how long you used the web site and to document that you ended the account.

Web Log

Web Site:			
Ancestor's Name	Birth Date	Death Date	Spouse

Web Site:			
Ancestor's Name	Birth Date	Death Date	Spouse

Web Log

Web Site:			
Ancestor's Name	Birth Date	Death Date	Spouse

Web Site:			
Ancestor's Name	Birth Date	Death Date	Spouse

Web Log

	Web Site:		
Ancestor's Name	Birth Date	Death Date	Spouse

	Web Site:		
Ancestor's Name	Birth Date	Death Date	Spouse

Web Log

Web Site:			
Ancestor's Name	Birth Date	Death Date	Spouse

Web Site:			
Ancestor's Name	Birth Date	Death Date	Spouse

Web Log

	Web Site:		
Ancestor's Name	Birth Date	Death Date	Spouse

	Web Site:		
Ancestor's Name	Birth Date	Death Date	Spouse

Web Log

	Web Site:		
Ancestor's Name	Birth Date	Death Date	Spouse

	Web Site:		
Ancestor's Name	Birth Date	Death Date	Spouse

Web Accounts

Web Site:					
User Name	Password	$	Day Monthly Yearly	Start Date	End Date

Web Site:					
User Name	Password	$	Day Monthly Yearly	Start Date	End Date

Web Site:					
User Name	Password	$	Day Monthly Yearly	Start Date	End Date

Web Site:					
User Name	Password	$	Day Monthly Yearly	Start Date	End Date

Web Site:					
User Name	Password	$	Day Monthly Yearly	Start Date	End Date

Web Site:					
User Name	Password	$	Day Monthly Yearly	Start Date	End Date

Web Site:					
User Name	Password	$	Day Monthly Yearly	Start Date	End Date

Web Accounts

Web site:					
User Name	**Password**	**$**	**Day Monthly Yearly**	**Start Date**	**End Date**

Web site:					
User Name	**Password**	**$**	**Day Monthly Yearly**	**Start Date**	**End Date**

Web site:					
User Name	**Password**	**$**	**Day Monthly Yearly**	**Start Date**	**End Date**

Web site:					
User Name	**Password**	**$**	**Day Monthly Yearly**	**Start Date**	**End Date**

Web site:					
User Name	**Password**	**$**	**Day Monthly Yearly**	**Start Date**	**End Date**

Web site:					
User Name	**Password**	**$**	**Day Monthly Yearly**	**Start Date**	**End Date**

Web site:					
User Name	**Password**	**$**	**Day Monthly Yearly**	**Start Date**	**End Date**

Web sites to consider

ancestry.com
rootsweb.com
genealogy.com
familysearch.com
Cindy's list.com
findagrave.com
shipslist.com
ellisisland.org
castlegarden.org
Google Books
The National Archives

A few Search engines
Google.com
Yahoo.com
Bing.com
Internet Explorer
Fire Fox

    I have found that most <u>Historical Societies</u> have websites some have links to databases and information that can be useful.

    <u>Libraries</u> have of history Books and city directories. Some have genealogy information as well. You may be able to use inter library loan to obtain books from other libraries that you may not be able to go to.

Places to go and or to contact

National archives
Historical societies
Libraries
Court houses
<u>Cemeteries</u> associated with your ancestors
<u>Funeral homes</u> associated with the family you are researching
<u>If you have ancestors in a war</u> check out the web sites pertaining to their war and don't forget to look into the battle fields and national parks that are connected to that particular war. Some of them have monuments and information that may contain the name of your ancestor.

Notes

Notes

Made in the USA
Columbia, SC
02 February 2019